JOHANNES BRAHMS

SCHICKSALSLIED
SONG OF DESTINY

for Chorus and Orchestra
Op. 54

D0503898

Ernst Eulenburg Ltd

London · Mainz · Madrid · New York · Paris · Tokyo · Toronto · Zürich

JOHANNES BRAHMS

Schicksalslied (Song of Destiny), Op. 54

Despite the claims made on Brahms as a concert pianist, much of his practical experience of music-making until within sight of his forty-second birthday came with choirs. Even as a schoolboy on holiday with friends in the small country town of Winsen, nothing gave him more pleasure than conducting the local Men's Choral Society and arranging folk-songs for them to sing. His first official part-time professional appointment at the Court of Detmold from 1857-9 involved conducting the Court Choir, which on his own admission helped immeasurably when he started to write new part-songs for them, notably the *Marienlieder* cycle. As he put it to his close friend, Joachim: 'What a small amount of practical knowledge I have! My stuff is written far too unpractically.' Back home in Hamburg he wasted no time in forming a ladies' choir of his own to conduct, which in turn inspired a further spate of part-songs and solo quartets and duets. Nevertheless it was Vienna that gave him his widest experience of choirs and the choral repertory, first as director of its Singakademie throughout the winter season of 1863-4, when their achievements included the first performance in that city of Bach's *Christmas Oratorio*, and eventually from 1872-5, as conductor of the renowned Gesellschaft der Musikfreunde, for whose concerts he could call on the considerably larger Singverein (some 300 or so voices) as well as orchestra.

It was between the two Viennese appointments that most of his major choral works were written, starting with the *German Requiem*. The two notable exceptions were *Nänie* and *Gesang der Parzen*, both dating from the early 1880s. Way back in 1853 his friend and champion, Robert Schumann, had predicted: 'When once he lowers his magic wand over the massed resources of chorus and orchestra, we shall have in store for us wonderful insights into the secret of the spiritual world'. Clara Schumann recalled this prophecy in her diary after the première of the *German Requiem* in Bremen Cathedral on Good Friday, 1868, for it was on that occasion that the musical world at large recognized Brahms's full stature for the first time. Naturally he felt spurred to complete his cantata *Rinaldo* in 1868, besides also producing the *Liebeslieder Waltzes* for voices and piano duet (1868-9), the *Alto Rhapsody* (1869), the *Triumphlied* (1870-1) and the *Schicksalslied* (1868-71).

Though few musicians then alive had greater respect for established classical tradition, Brahms was a true romantic in that everything he wrote grew from his own personal experience. The urge to compose a Requiem had been with him ever since the attempted suicide of Robert Schumann in

1854, though it was not until his mother's death eleven years later that ideas began to take definite shape. The other choral works are also in their way a reflection of his own emotional life, whether his love for Vienna and all her seductive charms confessed in the *Liebeslieder Waltzes*, his ardent patriotism and belief in a new, united Germany found in the *Triumphlied*, or the more intimate revelations of the *Alto Rhapsody* and *Schicksalslied*.

To her diary Clara Schumann confided the belief that it was Brahms's brief, undeclared attachment to her own daughter, Julie, who loved another, that led him to a passage from Goethe's *Harzreise*, in which a lonely outcast beseeches divine succour, for his *Alto Rhapsody*. 'He called it his bridal song . . . this piece seems to me neither more nor less than the expression of his own heart's anguish' were her words.

As for the *Schicksalslied*, it is important to remember that he began it in 1868, the year of the *German Requiem*'s Bremen première, when the contrast of Elysian peace and the anguish of this world was a concept still very close to his heart. He discovered Friedrich Hölderlin's poem early one morning, while staying with his old friend, Albert Dietrich, a former pupil of Schumann. Though its inspiration came more from classical antiquity than the German bible of the *Requiem*, Brahms was instantly possessed by it. Dietrich relates that while on an expedition to the great naval port of Wilhelmshafen that same day, Brahms several times wandered off grave and silent from the rest of his friends on the beach to start making sketches. Getting the work into shape nevertheless proved as long and arduous a process as this composer's larger projects so often tended to be, and chiefly because of the ending. Though no orthodox believer, Brahams still felt unable to conclude with Hölderlin's bleak vision of perishing humanity. For him there had to be some consolation through the return of the idyllic Elysian opening, though whether or not with a repeat of the text he could not decide. It was his friend, Hermann Levi, conductor of the Karlsruhe Opera, who eventually persuaded him that his first plan of recalling only the material of the orchestral prelude was the more telling. Brahms at this time spent much of his leisure at nearby Lichtental, not far from Baden-Baden, where Clara Schumann had a holiday home. Accordingly it was Levi who conducted the première of the *Schicksalslied* at one of the Karlsruhe Philharmonic Society's concerts on 18 October, 1871, just two months before its publication by Simrock. The Vienna première followed on 21 January 1872, at one of the Gesellschaft der Musikfreunde concerts under its then director, Anton Rubinstein.

The one liberty with words Brahms felt compelled to take, for the sake of musical balance, was in repeating Hölderlin's shorter second section of the poem. Its wild climax, prompted by the poet's image as 'hurled like water from rock to rock, through the years down into the unknown', is still more dramatically intense the second time because raised a tone higher. The

Elysian opening section also includes much subtle word-painting, though characteristically Brahms prefers only to suggest 'fingers of the artist touch her sacred strings' by spread chords from the string section rather than introducing a harp. His orchestra is no larger or more exotic than any used by Beethoven. Nothing in the work is more beautiful than the gradual redawning of light in the orchestral postlude, not in E flat major as at the start, but in a luminous C major, gleaming as if with a halo.

Joan Chissell, 1979

JOHANNES BRAHMS

Schicksalslied, Op. 54

Obwohl Brahms bis fast zu seinem zweiundvierzigsten Geburtstag vor allem als Konzertpianist in Anspruch genommen wurde, beruhte seine praktische Erfahrung im Musizieren hauptsächlich auf seiner Arbeit mit Chören. Selbst als er noch zur Schule ging und seine Ferien mit Freunden in der kleinen ländlichen Stadt Winsen verbrachte, kannte er kein grösseres Vergnügen, als den dortigen Männergesangverein zu dirigieren, und für ihn Volkslieder zu bearbeiten. Seine erste offizielle, wenn auch nicht vollbeschäftigte Stelle am Detmolder Hof von 1857 bis 1859 als, unter anderem, Dirigent des Hofchors, half ihm ausserordentlich, wie er selbst zugab, als er begann, für diesen Chor neue Lieder, darunter vor allem den Zyklus der *Marienlieder*, zu schreiben. Seinem nahen Freunde Joachim teilte er mit, wie wenig beträchtlich sein praktisches Wissen sei, und dass sein Zeug viel zu unpraktisch geschrieben wäre. Nach Hamburg zurückgekehrt, verlor er keine Zeit, seinen eigenen Frauenchor zu bilden und zu dirigieren, der ihn dann seinerseits dazu inspirierte, eine weitere Vielzahl von mehrstimmigen Gesängen, Soloquartetten und Duetten zu schreiben. Doch sammelte er erst in Wien den grössten Teil seiner Erfahrung mit Chören und mit ihrem Repertoire, zunächst als Leiter der Singakademie während der ganzen Wintersaison von 1863/64, in der als besondere Leistung die Wiener Erstaufführung des *Weihnachtsoratoriums* von Bach zu nennen ist, und schliesslich, von 1872 bis 1875, als Dirigent der berühmten Gesellschaft der Musikfreunde, für deren Konzerte ihm auch der wesentlich grössere Singverein (mit ungefähr 300 Stimmen), sowie das Orchester, zur Verfügung stand.

Seine hauptsächlichsten Chorwerke, angefangen mit dem *Deutschen Requiem*, schrieb Brahms in der Zeit, die zwischen den beiden, von ihm bekleideten Wiener Stellungen lag. Zwei bedeutende Ausnahmen waren *Nänie* und der *Gesang der Parzen*, die aus den frühen achtziger Jahren stammen. Schon im Jahre 1853 hatte sein Freund und Fürsprecher Robert Schumann vorausgesagt: ‚Wenn er seinen Zauberstab dahin senken wird, wo ihm die Mächte der Massen, im Chor und Orchester, ihre Kräfte leihen, so stehen uns noch wunderbarere Einblicke in die Geisterwelt bevor.‘ Clarä Schumann erinnerte sich an diese Weissagung und schrieb davon in ihrem Tagebuch nach der Uraufführung des *Deutschen Requiems* im Bremer Dom am Karfreitag 1868, denn bei diesem Anlass erkannte die gesammte musikalische Welt zum ersten Mal Brahms in seiner ganzen Grösse. Selbstverständlich wurde er dadurch angespornt, seine Kantate *Rinaldo* im Jahre 1868 zu vollenden, und ausserdem die *Liebeslieder-Walzer* für Gesangstimmen und vierhändiges Klavier (1868-9), die *Alt-*

Rhapsodie (1869), das *Triumphlied* (1870-1) und das *Schicksalslied* (1868-71) zu komponieren.

Obgleich Brahms für die eingewurzelte klassische Tradition mehr Respekt hatte, als die meisten damals lebenden Musiker, war er doch eine echter Romantiker, da alles was er schrieb, aus seinem eigenen Erleben erwuchs. Schon seit Robert Schumanns Selbstmordversuch im Jahre 1854, hatte Brahms den Drang empfunden, ein Requiem zu schreiben, doch dauerte es noch bis zu dem elf Jahre später erfolgten Tod seiner Mutter, bevor die musikalischen Ideen begannen, eine endgültige Gestalt anzunehmen. Auch die anderen Chorwerke gaben auf ihre Art sein eigenes Gefühlsleben wieder, ob es sich dabei um die *Liebeslieder-Walzer* handelte, in denen er seine Liebe für Wien und seinen ganzen verführerischen Charm bekannte, um seine glühende Vaterlandsliebe und seinen Glauben an ein neues, einiges Deutschland, die im *Triumphlied* ihren Ausdruck fanden, oder um die intimeren Bekenntnisse in der *Alt-Rhapsodie* und dem *Schicksalslied*.

Ihrem Tagebuch vertraute Clara Schumann an, sie glaubte, es wäre Brahms' kurzfristige, unerklärte Liebe für ihre eigene Tochter Julie, die einen anderen liebte, gewesen, welche ihn für seine *Alt-Rhapsodie* zu einer Stelle in Goethes *Harzreise* führte, in der ein einsamer Ausgestossener um göttliche Hilfe bittet. Sie berichtete weiter, dass er es sein Brautlied nannte, und dass ihr dieses Stück nichts mehr oder weniger als der Ausdruck seiner eigenen Herzensangst zu sein schien.

Was das *Schicksalslied* anbetrifft, so darf man nicht vergessen, dass Brahms diese Komposition 1868 begonnen hat, in dem Jahre also, in dem das *Deutsche Requiem* in Bremen uraufgeführt wurde, und in einer Zeit, in der ihm der Gegensatz zwischen einem elysischen Frieden und den Ängsten dieser Welt noch sehr am Herzen lag. Er entdeckte Friedrich Hölderlins Gedicht in einer frühen Morgenstunde, als er sich bei seinem alten Freund Albert Dietrich, einem früheren Schüler von Schumann, aufhielt. Obwohl es mehr von der klassischen Antike als von der deutschen Bibel des *Requiems* inspiriert ist, wurde Brahms auf der Stelle von diesem Gedicht gefesselt. Dietrich erzählt, wie Brahms noch am selben Tag, während eines Ausflugs zum grossen Flottenstützpunkt Wilhelmshafen, mehrmals ernst und schweigend seine Freunde verliess, um am Strand seine ersten Skizzen zu machen. Trotzdem erwies sich die Arbeit an der Gestaltung dieses Werks als so lang und mühsam, wie es die grösseren Projekte dieses Komponisten so oft zu verlangen schienen, und das vor allem des Schlusses wegen. Wenn Brahms auch nicht im orthodoxen Sinne gläubig war, so fühlte er sich doch nicht in der Lage, mit Hölderlins trostloser Vision vom Untergang der Menschheit zu schliessen. Für sich selbst brauchte er eine Art von Trost durch die Wiederholung des idyllisch elysischen Anfangs, doch konnte er sich nicht entscheiden, ob das mit oder ohne Wiederholung des Texts geschehen sollte. Schliesslich war es der Dirigent der Karlsruher Oper, sein Freund Hermann Levi, der ihn davon überzeugte, dass sein ursprünglicher Plan, nur die Musik des Orchestervorspiels zu wiederholen, der ausdrucksvollere war. Zu dieser Zeit verbrachte Brahms einen guten Teil seiner freien Zeit im nahem Lichtental, unweit Baden-Baden, wo Clara Schumann ein Ferienheim besass. So war es denn auch Levi, der die Uraufführung des *Schicksalslieds* in einem Konzert der Karlsruher Philharmonischen Gesellschaft am 18. Oktober 1871 dirigierte, und gerade zwei Monate später wurde das Werk schon von Simrock herausgegeben. Die Wiener Premiere folgte am 21. Januar 1872 in einem Konzert der Gesellschaft der Musikfreunde, unter der Leitung des damaligen Direktors Anton Rubinstein.

Die einzige Freiheit, die sich Brahms dem Text gegenüber gezwungen sah zu nehmen, war dass er, um des musikalischen Gleichgewichts willen, den zweiten, kürzeren Teil des Gedichts wiederholte. Der leidenschaftliche Höhepunkt, inspiriert durch das Bild des Dichters vom fallenden, Wasser von Klippe zu Klippe geworfen, jahrlang ins Ungewisse hinab', ist dennoch das zweite Mal intensiver, weil er einen Ton höher steht. Auch der elysische Anfang enthält viel feinsinnige Wortmalerei. Doch ist es charakteristisch für Brahms, dass er es vorzog, ,die Finger der Künstlerin heilige Saiten rührend', nur durch arpeggierte Akkorde der Streicher anzudeuten, anstatt eine Harfe zu verwenden. Sein Orchester ist weder grösser noch exotischer als das von Beethoven. Nichts ist im ganzen Werk schöner als das allmählich wiederkehrende Licht im Orchesternachspiel – nicht, wie anfangs, in Es-Dur, sondern in einem leuchtenden C-Dur, das glänzt, als wäre es von einem Heiligenschein umgeben.

Joan Chissell, 1979
Deutsche Übersetzung Stefan de Haan

Schicksalslied

Ihr wandelt droben im Licht
Auf weichem Boden, selige Genien!
Glänzende Götterlüfte
Rühren Euch leicht,
Wie die Finger der Künstlerin
Heilige Saiten.

Schicksallos, wie der schlafende
Säugling, atmen die Himmlischen;
Keusch bewahrt
In bescheidner Knospe
Blühet ewig
Ihnen der Geist,
Und die seligen Augen
Blicken in stiller,
Ewiger Klarheit.

Doch uns ist gegeben
Auf keiner Stätte zu ruhn;
Es schwinden, es fallen
Die leidenden Menschen
Blindlings von einer
Stunde zur andern,
Wie Wasser von Klippe
Zu Klippe geworfen,
Jahrlang ins Ungewisse hinab.

Friedrich Hölderlin

Song of Destiny

You roam aloft in radiance
with softness underfoot, ye blessed spirits!
Gleaming divine breezes
lightly touch you,
as the fingers of the artist
touch her sacred strings.

Free of Fate, like a sleeping babe,
the celestial beings breathe;
chastely preserved
in modest bud,
their souls
bloom eternally,
and their blissful eyes
gaze in calm
perpetual clarity.

But to us it is given
to find no resting-place;
suffering mankind
dwindles and falls
blindly from one hour
to the next,
hurled like water
from rock to rock,
through the years down into the unknown.

Friedrich Hölderlin
translation by Lionel Salter

SCHICKSALSLIED

(Friedrich Hölderlin)

Johannes Brahms, Op. 54
1833-1897

2

EE 6690

4

6

14

EE 6690

18

125
Fl.
Ob.
Cl. (B♭)
Fg.
Cor. (C)
Tr. (C)
I II Tbni. III
Timp.
S.
A.
T.
B.
I Vl. II
Vla.
Vc.
Cb.
cresc.
-len die lei - den - den, lei - - den-den Men - schen

27

EE 6690

EE 6690

36

EE 6690

EE 6690

38

40

wie Was - ser von Klip - pe zu Klip - pe

EE 6690

42

43

EE 6690

46

48

EE 6690

50

EE 6690

EE 6690

52